THE
WRITER'S BLOCK
TAROT

Vivian Caethe
Art by Amber Peter

Cuppatea Publications
2017

First Printing: 2017

ISBN 978-0-692-80497-1

Cuppatea Publications
Fort Collins, CO

www.viviancaethe.com

ACKNOWLEDGEMENTS

We would like to thank everyone who made this project possible. We are grateful for all our backers and supporters in this endeavor.

NOVELIST

Jacquline Hopson and Joy Dawn Johnson

COLLECTOR

Isidore Nettleship, Tina Noe-Good, Audrey Adams, Amber Beasley, Michael McAllister, Jack D Johnson, and Jenna L. Skeen

FRIEND

Toby Trask, Mia Kleve, Jake and Beverly Coutts, Jayme Pangalangan, Danielle Brigante, Todd Waggoner, Mark Greenberg, Nicole Sallak Anderson, Francisca & James Small, Nikki Rose-Royce, Andy Kwong, ESP, and Toby A Pugh

KING

Rebecca Varnum, Bex, Ashley Bourgeois, Courtney, Katelyn Sweigart, Ivy Hope, Holly Heisey, jaymi elford, Kim Switzer, Shawn Scarber, Eugene Kim, Eric Kent Edstrom, Barbara Jacksha, Robert J. McCarter, Ellen Sandberg, Travis Heermann, J. A. Campbell, Patience Virtue, Aaron Michael Ritchey, Dave Heyman, Sarah Mack, Peter 'Malkira' Lennox, Ann Z, Amanda Faith, Do Phuoc Duy, Tim "Kleehv" Shirk, Jesse, March, Keri Bas, Abby Kraft, Anthony Dobranski, Erik Justin Peterson, Lisa Webb, H. E. Strickon, Aleshia Howell, Ian Dominey, L.J. Hachmeister, Diane Wilkes, Kimberly Fordham, William R.D. Wood, Justine Jones, Joshua Otterholt, Ty Barbary, Dan Pierson, Script printing, Kim Le Patourel, TK Davis, Jadzia DeForest, Kirsten Porter, Ronin Lore, Cody Thompson, Jennifer

P. Wick, Jorja H., Matthew Millard Falco, Deputy, Carly Lanners, Scott Edwards, Dracos, William J Rooks, Hunter Price, Adie Rombach, Mark N Ziff, Ms Gypsy, Susan Adami, Lissette Evans, Katlyn Coyette, J.T. Evans, Patrick Hester, Raine Wy, K Parker, Victoria D. Morris, Peter Hollinghurst, Tarosophy Tarot Association, Gregory Block, Olivia San, Heidi A. Wilde, Rebecca Sczepanski, NinjAnna Doddridge, D Taylor-Rodriguez, Trystan Vel, Sherrie Miranda, Author, Shauna Roberts, Ashen Knight, Leslie Ellen Jones, B.J. West, Michael Scott Mears, Brian Bohn, MK Sauer. Joe Perri, Beverly Sandberg, Brenda M. Hardw, Soli Johnson, Deidri Deane, Matt Perry, Neil Carty, Joseph Schonbok, Jill Vassilakos-Long, Gregory Miranda, Gina Drayer, Gail W-V, Danny Pettry II, Scott, Hans Brinker, Tristan Luyks, Bur, Sean M. Locke, M. Lynne Lightowler, Dr. K-Two, Walter F. Croft, Anne Barringer, John Iovine, Shane Coineandubh, Bruce Dunn, Fritz, Brian S Weis, Rhel ná DecVandé, Peter Farrar, Mekhaela Jackson, @thoughtfulrat, Mystic Al, Ruth Ann Harnisch, Michele Hsu, Wendy Reijnhoudt, Patricia Welsh, Marjorie-Ann Garza, Sam Handley, Robert E. Stutts, Thomas Corbi, Wiyogo karta, Keira Marti: Maven of the Metaphysical, Cheryl Vogel, Clarity Beaumont, Rebecca Kratz, Sarina Rhoads, Jaime Wurth, Pamela Novotny, KK KAMINAKA, Mandy, Debi Hall, Regis Jack, M. V. Ho, Heather Baker, Aurich, Fred L Hammond, Shannon Sofian, Anita, Sean and Nicole Tubridy, Jeanne Scharfenberg, Joel and Melissa Palmer, Kyle Milner, Emilia Witthuhn, Siri, Mel DeLaGarza, Rebecca F, Ginger Scoggin, Lisa Walker England, George Buckner, Erica Eden Myles, Nicole Seefeldt, Jay Zastrow, Barbara Nova, Katherine Raclin, Danica West, Kelli Rubin, Genéa L. Michael, Reshma, Wes Macnamara, RoseRed Robinson, Matthew Curry, Megan Arnold, Shannon, D. M. M. Gurfein, Debra Metzger, Leron Culbreath, Mitch

Rigger, Luke 'PunQuillity' Elias, Inna Yakubova, Sueage, Akroma McAngelface, Merellus, Richard 'Vecna' Hussey, Demetri Jagger, Teresa Horne, Tabitha Redente, Rafael A. Pacheco, Alicia McKin, Monsieur LeBlanc, Margaret S. McGraw, AlmostHuman, Chris Fielding, Lee & Liza Wolff-Francis, Kevin Brum, Dan Hillen, Nate Taylor, Faengz, A. Gray, Mandy Rosevear, Morgan N Southworth, Leon, Kaethe Doherty, Jamie C. Fradelos, Manny Tears, Cheryl DF09, Mark Sable, Beverly, Mandy Wilkerson, Pete Evans, Stephen Clarke-Keating, Tessa Stransky, Stephan Lamoureux, Lee Currie, Mystic Lamb, Jay Shields, Sharan Volin, TJ Wilkes, Gerri J Hobdy, Joseph Philips, Nick Davis, L.K. Feuerstein, Bridgette R. Mag Aoidh, Nick Sutcliffe, Kyle Saritelli, Ramsey, Tyler Schrodt, Mike Tryon, Sunshine MorningRae, Merrilee~, Paxaday Marrow, Sherridan Green, Laurie Hicks, Kathleen, Barry Bailey, Damon-Eugene Rich, Gregory Loselle, Jacqui B., Angela Parr, Lilah Wild, Barbara Bordalejo, L. Messina, Fred Herman, Fred J. Chang, Betsy J, Charlie, Daniel Grizzle, Catherine Haines, Adrian Zollinger, Katie Harwood, George C Alexander, Allison Wisniewski, KT Wagner, Genevieve Slunkam, Johanna Hill, J. D. Gray, Michael Hicks, Menno Hansen, Jeremy Kear, Shoshana H. Reed, Kitty Quinn, Billy E Greer III, M.E. Gainey, Iretta Parks, Nathan "Moonbeast" Skank, D Patrick Beckfield, Ria Dunkley, Shoshanah Holl, Regan Marie Brown, Dakota Graves, Erin E. Parsons, Syne, Kelsa, Nikki Ebright, Amber Bibb, Madeline White, Eliaz McMillan, TC, Joyce Ann Garcia from McAllen, Tx., Jacob Ian Hiatt, Tammy Patterson, Eva, Signe Lyborg, Janne Potter, Asher Ling, Laurie Lamar, Martha Pratt, MikesMind, Wendy Hartley, Daijo, Jack Gulick, Kim Riek, Yu Tsai Su, John B. McCarthy, Tanya Spackman, S. Frazier, Pete Thu, Jane Kubel, Hoshi Aona, Felicia Fredlund, Jessica Flores, Chris & Erin Damm, Erisyuuki V., Ta'et Zahhat,

DL Birdwell, Derek Nejedlo, Trista Steele, Anastasia Thompson, Ant O'Reilly, Steve Fletcher, Porter Wiseman, Anthony Wendel, Anthony C Mackaronis, Steven Hall, Anne van de Wijdeven, AJ Nordall, Carl E. Martin, Kate Monster, Jodi Greenfelder, Lance Hurst, Dever Baophel, Andrea Eastman, Sham Suri, Spamdesu, Evan Camomile, Linda Smit Poche, Akayana, Tracy F., Anthony "Naz" Iannazzi

QUEEN

Sid Orlando, N.L. Riviezzo, Aleen Simms, NVMcDonald, Wendy (Pairaka) Lee, Risa Wolf, Khadeja Merenkov, Janet Rose, Lindsey M Cannan, Jennifer C., Erik Perez, Annie Smith, Andrew, Holly Pickett, Paul Winger, Addy Street, Christopher hagensick, Sam Billington, Yvonne Law, Melissa Anderson, J.A. Miller, Jeffrey Parkin, Robin D. Owens, John Fiala, Merle Joy Turchik, Brad Roberts, Greg Bennett, Ruth Ames, Stant Litore, L. Gregory, MJ Foley, Gabe Kinsman, Gini Von Courter, Jen Moore, Brian LeRoy Dahlstrom, Kelly Rede, Spring Lenox, Gabriella Herkert, Ilja Preuß, Lisa H., Sarah Kingdred, Tracy Rowan, lisa dee port white, Samantha Bloom, Rosie Lee, Rachel Heinrich, Michael A. Arnzen, Gonzalo Figueroa - CNG Studios, Victoria Martin, Denise Poepping, Josh K., BA Flowers, Erin Co, Eric Thomas Juzgrey, Andrew D'Agostino, Sheila M. Lane, Samuel D Feris, Roslind Sanders, Jaclyn N. Brassell, Tiffany Wright, Joe Wright, Brent M Persun, Wesley Lucas, Bismarck Frate, Hannah Moody, Mark Brumbill, Lalia Wilson, Rhianna Walker, Sandra Ruff-Blackington, Linda Cota, Michael Kaiser, Janka Hobbs, Marisa Mangione, Joe Schelin, Mx. Tiffany Leigh, Lori Brooks, Letha Matthews, Samuel Stoute, Judith Neidorff, Anita Olin, Alison Hunter

KNIGHT

Keith R.A. DeCandido, robgonzo, Eva Solar, Brook &
Julia West, Douglas Harmon, Ronaldo J, Jami Good,
and Rubiee Tallyn Hayes

PAGE

Martin Greening, David Perlmutter, Helen Savore, Lisa
Millraney, Stephanie Brown, Stefani Michelle, Thomas
Kapitza, DreamClassier, Thomas A. Fowler, Jenny Son,
Jan Avende, Zoë Steel, James Dearing, Prince Grevin,
Shana Rose MacKinnon, R. A. Z. Imhoff, Katrina L.
Halliwell, Viannah E. Duncan, and Klaudia Wixted

CONTENTS

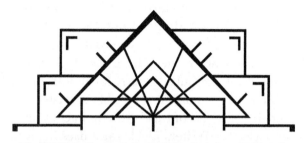

INTRODUCTION: THE WRITER'S BLOCK TAROT

Tarot is a means of interpreting our lives through the context of images and concepts that speak to the deeper parts of our psyche. From a psychological perspective, it whispers to the inner focus of our collective subconscious, the same well from which writers, poets, artists, and others draw their inspiration. Using archetypes and common concepts, it allows the viewer, the reader, as well as the author to find deep commonalities between the stories they write and the stories they live.

The Writer's Block Tarot is a guide for the writer to delve deeper into the writing process. It serves as an inspiration to flesh out their character's actions and motivations. It may also be used like a traditional tarot for the individual seeking to understand their lives with a fresh viewpoint, through a writer's perspective.

I have been using tarot and reading for others for over ten years. During that time, I have often recommended that authors use tarot to explore their stories and what impulses drive them to write the stories they do. Such exercises revealed a need for a tarot designed for writers.

Although there is no tarot specifically geared to helping writers with their craft, the most commonly used tarot, the Rider–Waite, follows the Hero's Journey model. I have used this deck as inspiration, and subsequently break it from the Hero's Journey to make it accessible to writers and readers in all stages of their growth. In contrast to other decks, the Writers Block Tarot uses in particular the language and symbolism of the writer's craft, making it apt particularly for the writer.

Tarot is commonly considered to be many things, from a tool for fortune telling to a psychic guide, to a glimpse into the future. Although it can be those steadfast stand–ins, it can also be a window to the conscious and subconscious aspects of our experience as humans. In Jungian thought, the tarot uses images and archetypes to draw upon emotions and impressions that encourage the mind to draw connections between past experience, current situations, and future projections. Not coincidentally, writing also uses images and archetypes to express meaning through words and concepts.

Archetypes in particular work as emotional and conceptual shorthand that allow people to share stories and experiences. For example, we have the Adversary in the Antagonist and the Caregiver in Growth. The tarot builds off of these archetypes and transcends them by using them obviously and subtly in each card. As with life, each card has layers of meaning that gives a story depth and breadth.

The tarot is traditionally broken up into two sections: the Major Arcana and the Minor Arcana. The Major is composed of twenty–two cards, numbered zero to twenty–one. The Minor is comprised of fifty–six cards and is related to the modern playing cards. The Minor have the pip cards, numbered one through ten, along with the court cards: Page, Knight, Queen, and King. In most tarot the Major Arcana are given more weight, speaking to larger concepts, while in the Minor Arcana, smaller and less world–shaking concepts are played out.

In the Writer's Block Tarot, the Major Arcana represent larger aspects of the plot and characters that the protagonist(s) experience as they go through the story. The Minor Arcana represent the detailed aspects around them that can influence the plot, both conceptually and directly.

The pages for each card are intended to illuminate the meaning of each card. An introduction is followed by questions to consider and finally keywords that can briefly convey the general meaning of each card. When drawing a card, it may appear upright or reversed, depending on how it was shuffled. The orientation of the card conveys its own particular meaning. A right side up card's meaning is intended to convey the "loyal" meaning of the card (how it is represented in the spread in relationship to the other cards) versus the upside down or "disloyal" meaning of the card. This is similar to the concept of the synonym and antonym of a word, only think of it as it applies to the character. Loyalty and disloyalty in this case refer to the innate meaning of the card and how well it is conveyed in the situation in which it is placed.

The main focus of tarot is characters and characterization of their journey through the story (whether for actual humans, or fictional characters). When using this deck for writing, consider doing a reading for each major character, not just the main character. Even the villain is the protagonist in their own story. Use this deck to develop all the characters and explore their stories. Think beyond the basic story and delve deeper into the backstories, the hidden stories, and even the archetypal traits that can add vibrancy and life to the story. The deeper you go with this deck, the greater your understanding of your work will be.

The Writer's Block Tarot can be used for stories at all parts of their development, whether they are finished and in the editing stage, mid–draft, or barely begun as thoughts. Use the cards as ways to develop an existing plot, work through issues with current character arcs, develop stories, and anything else you can imagine.

In addition, this deck can be used to examine elements of worldbuilding. Consider the overall consequences of the world as it's represented in the cards and how these factors would play out in the universe created through the writing process.

As with any tarot deck, or any book, the interpretation is up to the reader, not the creator. If my definitions work work, then use them. If not, use this deck and book in any way that will best help you grow as a writer.

THE HISTORY OF TAROT

According to historians, the earliest documented mentions of the tarot emerged in the fifteenth century in Italy, tied to the Visconti family during the Italian Renaissance[1]. Although there have been French decks purported to be older, there is little evidence to substantiate this claim.[2] Rather, it is thought that the concept of playing cards was possibly brought over to Sicily from the Arabic cultures during the 1300s.[3] The tarot then evolved from this original card game and began to be played in the 1430s and later.[4] The central hub of cities where the game of tarot was played was Milan, Ferrara, Bologna, and Florence.[5]

Unlike modern tarot, the Italian decks were solely used as a playing card game but possess the structure that we are familiar with today, including the standard pip cards (numbered ten–one), the face cards (king, queen, knight, and knave), the fool (the wild card), and the twenty-one trump cards.[6] When played, the trump cards would be used in such a way as to allow the player to trump the last player's card if they held a card of a higher value, much like bridge today.[7]

Some of the surviving decks from this era are called the Visconti, Visconti–Sforza, and the Brera-Brambilla. These decks were likely painted in the workshop of Bonifacio Bembo.[8] It is believed that they were commissioned by Filippo Maria Visconti and his son in law Francesco Sforza and many cards from each deck are still extant in museums today.[9] Tarot historian Helen Farley theorizes that this is the origin of the tarot deck, as many of the iconography of the major arcana can be associated with aspects of the Visconti history and the culture of the era. An example of this would be The Popess, which is thought to be based off the "Pope Joan" stories of the era, as well as a woman related to the Viscontis, Sister Maifreda da Priovano, who for a time was, in some eyes, a spiritual leader akin to a pope and in other eyes a heretic.[10]

In contrast to the Visconti deck (which included the theological virtues and other cultural symbols of Renaissance Italy along with other variations), the Visconti–Sforza deck most resembles modern decks.[11] The list of trump cards in the latter deck is "the world, followed by the angels... the sun, moon, star, temperance, death, traitor, old man, wheel of fortune, fortitude, chariot, justice, love, pope, emperor, popess, empress, and mountebank, followed by the fool."[12]

The concept of trumps may have arisen from the "triumphs" and the I Trionfi poem by Petrarch, which were an integral part of cultural under-standing during the Renaissance. In the art and poem from this era, it was not uncommon to see

the virtues represented as if in a parade. Some
theorists have correlated this concept with the
order of the trumps, and how each trump rises
from the next.[13]

From Italy, the game spread to many of the Euro-
pean countries of the era, except for the British
Isles.[14] In the later centuries, up to the mid–1700s,
the decks changed depending on the area, evolving
from the traditional Renaissance styles to local
imagery and taking on French names for the suits
(rather than Swords, Cups, Coins, and Batons,
the suits became Spades, Hearts, Diamonds, and
Clubs).[15] Also intended as a card game, the Tarot
de Marseille originated in the 17th century and is
the oldest still printed decks still being printed (the
most recent edition released by Phillipe Camoin
and Alejandro Jodorowsky).[16]

Divination with playing cards (cartomancy)
came into popular use in the 1700s with the Piquet
pack of playing cards.[17] Robert Place, however,
argues that the tarot could have also been used
in the fifteenth century for divination, but not in
the manner of the eighteenth century. Rather, he
argues that the art of the Italian cards represented
a mystical shorthand that could have been used for
spiritual purposes.[18]

During this 1700s , however, the tarot had
remained as a provincial game, but was for the
most part forgotten in Paris[19]. The occultists of
this era, however, rediscovered the tarot through
the writings of Antoine Count de Gébelin, who
was the first to state that the tarot's origins came
from Egypt. This seems unlikely as none of the
symbolism of the prior tarot decks had any ties to
Egyptian culture and were predominantly Euro-

pean and Christian in provenance.[20]

More likely is the interest of Gébelin and his contemporaries in the Egyptomania of the era due to Napoleon's excursions into the area and his subsequent return with priceless artifacts from Egypt. The mystery and allure of Egypt's history (both actual and mythologized) inspired French imagination and informed generations of occultists in development of their magical systems. This perpetuation of the myth of Egyptian origins is often considered by some to be a search for authenticity as well as an exotication of the tarot beyond its origins in Italy[21].

Following Gébelin. Jean–Baptiste Alliette (known as Etteila) began using the tarot deck for divination purposes as well.[22] To make the correspondences he felt were needed, Etteila created "The Book of Thoth" tarot deck based on theories of Hermeticism and also claimed Egyptian provenance. Etteilla's deck is one of the first to modify the existing playing card deck to a more arcane purpose.[23] In his version, he revised the order of the trumps and made changes to some of their subjects.[24]

The next tarot student to make a change, Éliphas Levi argued against the Egyptian theory and formed a syncretism between various occult schools of thought, tying the tarot to the Kabbalah and other magical traditions[25]. In contrast to Etteila, Levi theorized that the now–called "major arcana" tied into the twenty–two letters of the Hebrew alphabet, and reordered the trumps to correspond by placing the Magician at the beginning and the Fool after Judgment but before The World.[26]

Papus, in his *Le Tarot des Bohémiens: Le Plus Ancien Livre du Mondei*, further perpetuated these theories in 1889 by also claiming the tarot came about as knowledge from the "gypsies" and also from India and Egypt. He also expanded on the correspondences between Tarot and the Kabbalah.[27]

When the tarot made its way to England, it finally blossomed into the form we are most familiar with today. The members of the Hermetic Order of the Golden Dawn were primarily responsible for this form of the tarot, along with its final correspondences and meanings derived from kabbalah, Egyptian mythology, Freemasonry, and other occult sources. The Golden Dawn brought together many of the elements of occult society of the Victorian Era and their version of the tarot became a focal point of those beliefs and practices.[28]

The final evolution of the tarot came when A.E. Waite contracted Pamela Coleman Smith to paint his Rider–Waite deck.[29] Combining the esoteric traditions of Levi and the Golden Dawn, Waite created an innovative tarot deck that borrowed from past decks in construction but broke with them in design. While keeping the order developed by Levi and the Golden Dawn, the Rider–Waite–Smith deck was the first to incorporate images rather than symbols for the minor arcana.[30] To this date, many modern tarot decks use this format, and some of them even copy the same design elements while still making the deck thematically different.

Today there are thousands of tarot decks designed for a variety of purposes. Many, if not all, of them derive their inspiration from these original decks and the mythos surrounding them. With this deck, we are continuing a tradition that is hundreds of years in the making and that I hope will continue for many years to come.

HOW TO READ TAROT

There are as many ways to read tarot as there are people in the world. This section is not meant to be a rigid guide as to how to best read the cards, but rather an example of how I do it. The basic guidelines below are followed by a sample reading.

First, shuffle the cards. I recommend doing this with every reading, no matter if they were shuffled beforehand. This allows time to gather your thoughts. While doing so, figure out what you want to read for. Are you looking for a story structure? A way past a block? Ways to develop a character? Some of the spreads are specifically designed to address certain questions.

Divide them into three piles, and then select one pile. Reassemble the deck with that pile on top.

Deal the cards by flipping them from the top of the deck away from you and place them on your reading surface. This is where you will determine if they are loyal or disloyal, depending on how they are drawn. If you are interested in using a pattern, or spread, there are some in the back of this book. In these spreads, the position of the card in relationship to the others indicates an extra meaning that adds to the cards in relation to each other. If this seems too complex at first, work from the smaller one or three card spreads until you become more familiar with the process.

With a one card draw, simply look at the card and determine the meaning based on the explanations in this book. I suggest framing a question or a concept in your mind first.

If using a multiple card spread, once you have laid all the cards out, read the cards by interpreting the placement and meaning of the first card of the spread to the last. I often take notes as I go, writing down the card, its placement within the spread, and its meaning in the position it was dealt. When I was a novice at reading tarot, this helped me not only frame the reading in my mind, but also learn the meanings of the cards by writing them down.

To start, tell a story from the cards. Many of the complex spreads help in this process, but even a three card spread can tell a story or elucidate your own. Reading the cards in the order of the spread can help with this. For example, the most common three card spread is the Past/Present/Future spread and is read from left to right. Following the meaning of the cards should lay out a component of your story or a brand new story for you to work with.

After the reading is done, make notes about changes in your story and what you think will help you in the future.

THE MAJOR ARCANA

As mentioned before, the Major Arcana represent aspects of the plot, illustrating the character's path from the beginning of the story to the end. When drawing these in a reading, look at how they relate to the other cards and can explain parts of the story, either with the goal of improving parts of the story or shedding light on those parts that are currently being worked on.

Loyal: proactive movement, action, strong characters, moving forward, engagement, beginnings, the quest

Disloyal: reactive, inaction, weak characters, cardboard characters, stagnation, boredom, nothing new

0 • PROTAGONIST

We start this story with the Protagonist.

The character is the central figure as they begin their story. Are they central to the narrative, or a side character in their own story? Are they driven by the action, or are they indecisive and incapable of forward motion? The concept of action applies to all stories, even those that don't have literal action, but are inclined more toward character progression.

Whether the story has one main character or a cast of characters, the Protagonist of every scene must be central to the action or the conflict. The Protagonist leads the reader through the story, enticing them with what they might do and how they might grow. Readers read stories to find out what happens next on the characters' emotional and literal path through the narrative. In the reading of a book, the Protagonist is the skin the reader puts on to experience the world and the story.

When crafting the Protagonist's story, ponder where they are starting and where they are going to go. Sometimes the places the character goes are surprising to even the writer. When writing the story, re-evaluate the character's development on a regular basis to make sure they are in constant motion. The minute they stop moving, either action-wise or emotionally, the narrative dies. Keep the story alive by building the conflict and tension from page one to the climax of the story.

Loyal: learning, experience, news, situations, locations, setting, fire

Disloyal: hidden knowledge, closemindedness, inexperience, bigotry, naiveté, doldrums, white room

I • KNOWLEDGE

The Protagonist is ill-advised to continue within their story without knowledge or what they think is knowledge about their situation.

Knowledge informs the character's actions as they go forward, from the very beginning of the book to its end, but it should also inform your writing as you begin the story and write it to its conclusion. What about this story do you want to convey? How will your readers know and understand the story? Is there even enough knowledge to convey the message?

This knowledge can be more than what the character explicitly knows. Consider as well what they must implicitly know about their world and how to work within it. What makes their world and their experience with the world different from our own? What makes these things similar to our own?

With this knowledge also comes an understanding of what is needed to accomplish the task or begin the journey. What does your character need to succeed? What do they strive for? Knowing these things can also help your story grow and develop. If you do not know, stop and consider what they might be, since if you as the author don't know, the character is unlikely to know either.

Loyal: inciting incident, questions, excitement, mystery, challenge, air

Disloyal: disinterest, obviousness, unchallenging circumstances, false mystery, red herrings

II • MYSTERY

A mystery of any sort is the key to an engaging story, no matter how grand or small its scale. What about the story and the Protagonist's actions have engendered a mystery that keeps the reader going? These concepts encourage interest in the story by providing the final "why" to the other questions.

This triptych of cards, the Protagonist, Knowledge, and Mystery, provide the basis for any good story and the contents of the exposition. It includes the character, what they know, and what they want to know more about. The mystery is the initiation of conflict in that it is keeping the character from the satisfaction they crave or need.

With their sense of self and their knowledge, the character begins their journey toward the mystery that can tell them what they might become, who they might be, or how they will overcome the obstacles in their lives. It is your responsibility as the author to make this mystery so engaging that it draws not only the character, but also the reader through the story from beginning to end, while also making the reveal of the mystery as pleasing as possible.

The mystery at its inception is what makes the character question their place in life and their existence. It is the challenge that encourages them to be more than they currently are. It is the beginning of the quest that drives them past what they initially expected and makes them become more than they ever thought they could be.

Loyal: nurturing, adaptive development, change, water

Disloyal: stagnation, maladaptive development, stunted growth, poison, decay

III • GROWTH

For a character to move through the narrative, they must be able to grow. This growth can come from something within themselves or an external impetus toward growth and nurturing. These characteristics play into their character description and how they relate to the world around them.

When determining these factors, ask yourself: how does your character grow through the story? How do they want to grow? Does their growth and need to change come off as adaptive or maladaptive? Do they grow in spurts, or gradually?

All humans have things that feed their souls. What feeds your character's soul? What makes them want to grow and change? What do they nurture within themselves? What do they want to nurture within other people?

Consider for a moment how most people view nurturing. They tend to see it as a healthy thing, a happy thing. In many instances it is a healthy thing and should be honored.

In contrast, there are other kinds of nurturing. For example, consider the antagonist. What would they want to nurture? Is it something healthy that they don't know how to grow? Or are they so evil that they would want to grow something abominable in the world?

When crafting your character, consider what they want in their world and what their end–goal is, the world they want to create. What nurturing must they do for this to happen? What do they expect of the world and what will they fight for to gain this growth?

Loyal: support, mastery, power, control, stone, earth

Disloyal: over–controlling, manipulativeness, instability, lack of agency

IV • AGENCY

Each character must have agency within their own story. In order for a character to have agency, they need to have something they want and are willing to strive for. If growth is vital, agency provides the trellis for that growth. Characters strive to return the world to the stability they expect from it or change it to reflect what they want, but they often do not have the tools yet to make that happen when they begin the story. What tools do they make or receive during the story for them to be the person who can affect these changes? What do they learn that gives them the ability to support that which is most important to them? What provides them means to control aspects of their lives which they once had no control over?

When a character begins a story, they have very little agency to support the things that mean the most to them. This is why stories sometimes begin with the loss of that which must be regained. The character, in order to regain that thing, must learn to grow in these characteristics and use them in a manner that can support their goal, rather than hindering them.

Agency is often something that is earned through hard work by the character, not something they necessarily start out with. However, if they do not end the story with some level of agency, then the story has not been fully realized. Consider how your character gains control over their world in order to succeed at their goals.

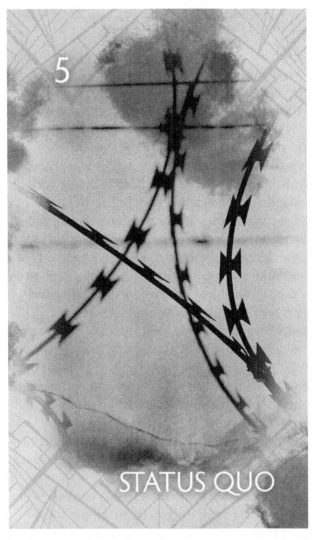

5

STATUS QUO

Loyal: normal, the way things are, the way things were, the way things should be

Disloyal: no sense of place or time, no world-building, no sense of the way things are, were, or should be

V • STATUS QUO

The status quo represents things as they are, whether the character likes it or not. This card moves us from the initial questions and character considerations to the setting of the story by asking: Where does it begin?

With a majority of stories, the narrative starts with the things as they are "now". Sometimes in the next few pages, that "now" is shattered into the conflict, or it begins in media res with the conflict front and center. The status quo can be the original "now" (before everything turned into the conflict) or it can be the "now" in which the present is the conflict and the characters must move through it to re-establish their ideal version of the status quo.

There are several things that are vital about this beginning (as well as other parts) of the story and the end-goal of the characters. If they align, then the entire novel must be guided to mirror the beginning and end of the narrative. If they are misaligned, then it is important to make sure that this is woven into the conflict as well.

Keeping all of these things in mind, consider where and how you want the character's story to start. How do you want to represent the status quo and in what manner would it be best revealed? What is the strongest place for this scene, this chapter, this story, or this novel to begin? What is "normal" and how will the character deal with that normal?

Loyal: passion, interest, desire, devotion
Disloyal: disinterest, broken heart, apathy, ennui

VI • LOVE

Love is something that all characters should have, but sometimes don't when not properly crafted. In this card, love is meant to represent more than their one true love or the object of their lust (although it can mean those things). Rather, it should be viewed in the larger context of the character's desires as a whole. What do they want most in life? Can they be said to love that thing?

Does that thing complete their life and give it meaning, or does it tear it down and make them miserable? Does it drive their quest onward, or does it distract them from their quest and make them lose their way?

When writing a character, ask what they love, and then how that love plays out in every aspect of their character. Does it help them or hinder them? Does it add to the conflict or ease it? Everyone loves something, and it is your job to discover what that is for your character, and, more importantly, write it in such a way that it becomes the important aspect of their life that it should be.

Once these questions have been answered, consider how this aspect ties into the other aspects of their characterization. How does it interact with Growth and Agency? How does it affect the Status Quo? And so forth. Love should impact all of these things and more, showing the depth of the character's passions and how far the character is willing to go to serve that desire. Start the book with those things and grow the character through these key concepts.

Loyal: Embarkation, travel, movement, development

Disloyal: Delays, stagnation, doldrums

VII • JOURNEY

In order for the plot to move forward, the character must move on from that status quo and the things they love. They have to step out of their comfort zone and embark on a journey, whether literal or metaphorical, to navigate the conflict and arrive at the climax of the story.

This can also reflect the pacing of the story. The way the journey is begun and enacted should indicate how quickly the story will move along. Is it an action story, a contemplative story, or something else entirely? If an action story, does the plot move quickly, or does it drag? Do the characters get through the conflict so quickly that tension is not established?

Another way to look at this card is the literal journey the character takes through the plot. What is their path on their quest through the story? Is it a literal path as they journey from one city to the next? Or is it a metaphorical transition from being one kind of person to being another kind of person?

In all of these ways, the key concept is movement, not stagnation. Once the story's beginning has been introduced, it must move forward if it is to engage the reader.

8

CONSEQUENCES

Loyal: action, reaction, response

Disloyal: boring outcomes, lack of conflict, falling flat

VIII • CONSEQUENCES

For every character movement, there should be a consequence, appropriate for the character action. Characters do not move within a void, and their decisions and actions should resonate throughout the story and have consequences that perhaps even they do not yet realize.

Keeping the consequences of the characters' actions always in mind can provide depth and complexity to a story, elevating it from a mere trip between A and B. These effects also tie into the conflict, deepening not only the understanding of it, but also the complexity of it, adding layers to the basic conflict.

Use this card to consider the ways actions can have reactions, both to the character and the plot. Also when considering these things, use all of the tools at your hand to contribute to strengthening the conflict. This should include the worldbuilding concepts that lend weight to the consequences of the actions within the specific context or universe of the story in question.

When writing the consequences of the character's actions and choices, be sure to match the magnitude to the action. A small action may have great consequences, but a large action should rarely have small consequences. When writing each action, what are the ramifications for the character, as well as the world through which they move? How do these actions affect the plot and the character's goals? Do they help or hinder the movement of the character through their journey? What does the character learn?

Loyal: mentor, life-changing experiences, growing up, guidance

Disloyal: deception, hindrances, delusions, false guides.

IX • GUIDE

Every character needs something to light the way, whether it be another character or an event. Most often the guide shows up soon after the beginning of the story, sometimes along the way of the journey or sometimes precipitating the journey itself. They not only can start the journey, but may also provide the testing ground where the character first learns how their actions can affect the world around them and what the consequences of taking those actions will be.

The most traditional example of this concept is Merlin, the character that trains and focuses the protagonist to be the best form of themselves that they can be. Is there a person who provides this function in the story?

When writing an event as a guide instead of a character, consider the formative events in your own life and how the event in question guides the character onto a path they might not have had the strength or knowledge to take on their own.

The interesting thing about the guide is the nature of the concept as both a propelling force and a hindering mass. Often the thing or person that forms the character can also be the biggest stumbling block once the character outgrows them.

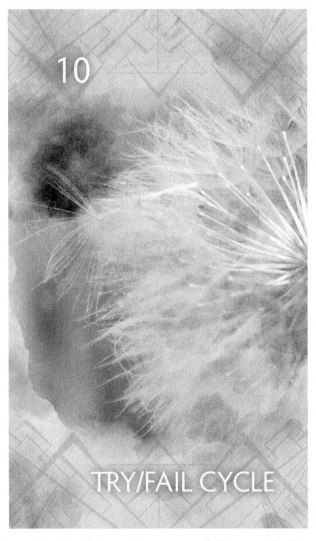

Loyal: struggles, cycles, success, failure, cyclical plot

Disloyal: ease of motion, lack of challenges, flat plot

X • TRY/FAIL CYCLE

This concept contains all the attempts the character makes to reach the end of the conflict, and their results. The traditional format involves three try/fail cycles as fewer seem too easy to believe and more seem to drag on, limiting the character's efficacy.

Every time the character attempts something and fails to complete it in a manner they would view as success, this is a try/fail. The purpose of these within the plot is not only to show the difficulty of the conflict, but also to show character growth. If a character completes an important task on the first try, what do they learn from it? Characters learn through adversity and the Try/Fail Cycle provides a form of that adversity for the character to be thrown onto the wheel and grow with every rotation.

The Try/Fail Cycle can be explicit within the story (where the character literally tries and fails three or so times in a row) or implicit (in the thought processes). No matter how it appears, character growth and development must spring forth from it. When examining your story, look at the number of times the character tries and see how often they succeed. Is their journey too easy? Do they succeed too readily at all tasks no matter the difficulty? Conversely, are their tasks too impossible to accomplish for the character as they are written? How many times must the character attempt a task before being able to succeed at it? How has this made them grow as a person?

11

STRENGTH

Loyal: strength, power, support, determination, ferocity

Disloyal: weakness, instability, lack of agency, frailty, passiveness

XI • STRENGTH

Strength is a trait that all characters should have, no matter their disposition or the way the strength presents itself in their development.

In fiction, strength tends to show up in ways that not only move the plot forward, but to give the character the ability to make the changes they need to in the world, or stand up to the changes others are making. Often the goal of strength is to create a new status quo or maintain the one they view as the best, most stable, version of the world.

When they gain the strength to make these changes, what about their worldview shifts to reflect this more stable world? The character's perception of themselves and their place within the world must change as the story changes as well. How do their perceptions of strength change? Does their strength mature, become deeper, more solid?

When writing a character's strengths, consider how each aspect of their personality can be a strength or a weakness. Play to those strengths, but also use their weaknesses to build tension throughout the story. Only by overcoming the challenges posed to their strengths and weaknesses can characters truly grow.

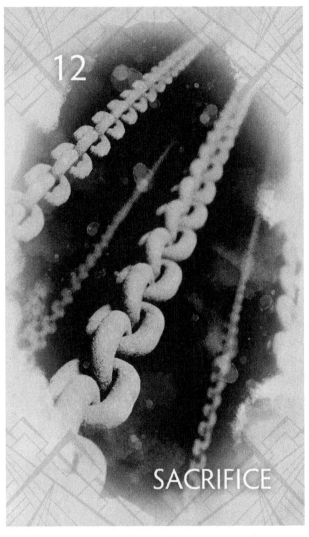

Loyal: hazards, pitfalls, challenges, derailments
Disloyal: easy obstacles, not challenging, security, ease

XII • SACRIFICE

In any good story, the character's path should be poorly paved and often treacherous. Sacrifices allow your story to keep moving and provide your characters with the impetus to change. Without sacrifice, the characters would never grow and the plot would become stale and anti–climactic.

Sacrifices can be inspired by actions of the antagonist, other characters, events in the world, or even the main character themselves. Look at the plot and determine where best the character can be sabotaged or self–sabotage themselves.

These hurdles shake the character's reality, making them look at things from a new perspective, often one that has challenged them or perhaps not even occurred to them before. It also can make them give up that which they think is the most important in their lives, only to discover that they didn't need it after all.

Another benefit of sacrifices to the character is the needed opportunity for them to re–examine their situation and way of living. Perhaps they have been doing the same thing they have always done with some success. When that thing becomes no longer successful, they must reevaluate their lives and their means of accomplishing the task at hand. They must sacrifice the routine to grow.

No matter the nature of the sacrifice, it must be sufficiently daunting so as to prevent the character from easily acceding to it. When writing these, ask whether they accomplish this task. Also determine whether they add to the plot or distract from it.

Loyal: change, revolution, chrysalis, death to current self

Disloyal: stagnation, decay, quiescence, sameness

XIII • TRANSFORMATION

For every character to progress through their arc, they must transform from what they once were to what they must be. This can mean the complete transformation of the character from one state to the next (young adult to adult, wife to widow, and so forth) or the small transformation of the character's personality and actions. Often when the transformation is completed and the story is near its end, the character may look back and realize they barely recognize their former self.

This transformation may take its form as a status (peasant to king), an emotion (hopeful to disappointed), mental status (un-medicated to treated), or even physical (injured to healed). Each of these moves the character from one state to the next, often several times or over the course of the story.

Consider too how this transformation may have to come through the actions of the character, when they are forced to change. Does this transformation make them the person they always wanted to be, a different person from that which they had always imagined, or even the very thing they never wanted to be? Determine how your character will transform and the ramifications of this transformation.

What factors will force their transformation? How do they deal with these changes and to what degree do they allow themselves to be transformed? Is this transformation for the better or worse?

14

BALANCE

Loyal: temperance, careful plotting, ease, stability
Disloyal: disruption, sloppy plotting, imbalance, strain, teetering

XIV • BALANCE

Balance is integral to every story in so many ways it's hard to count them all. When writing, consider carefully how the elements within the narrative and the universe coordinate to provide a coherent story. Some stories can benefit from unbalanced structures, especially if the intent is to create a sense of unease or discomfort for the reader, but with the vast majority of stories, the elements of the story should be balanced so that the reader barely notices them as they read. The more balanced the attention given to plot, characters, theme, setting and so forth, the more the story will flow. The more the story flows, the more enjoyable it is for the reader.

While the overall balance of the story is important, internal balance for the character is also important. Consider what makes the character tick and look at the forces affecting that. A character in balance is a character without stress. Look for ways your characters are balanced and unbalanced, set against that which opposes them from without and from within.

Also be wary of characters that lack balance in more ways than one. It is possible for a character to be too good or too evil, too perfect or too flawed.

When writing this part of the character's story, this is also a good place to provide them with the skills they need to control the balance in their lives. This is when all their previous experiences come to the fore and they begin to learn mastery.

Loyal: opposition, resistance, force, evil

Disloyal: weakness, cardboard characters, passive, helper disguised as an enemy

XV • ANTAGONIST

For every character, there must be an Antagonist, something or someone who strives to prevent them from achieving their goal. The Antagonist can be anything, from a person, to a force of nature, to even the character's own mind. But whatever the Antagonist is, be sure that it also is believable and provides the character with an opposing force. If the Antagonist is too weak, the protagonist becomes less believable and less interesting.

The Antagonist serves as the counterbalance to the protagonist, the character or concept that keeps the plot moving by providing opposition to the main character's goals. This makes them both extremely valuable and extremely vulnerable if they are not written as having goals of their own outside of the main character's needs..

When writing the Antagonist, regard them as a character in their own right, not just a thing which the Protagonist must oppose. Ask yourself, what are the Antagonist's motivations? How do they work to cross purposes with the protagonist's? What about them makes them tick? What is their story; the story in which they are the hero?

Loyal: tragedy, emergencies, failures, trials

Disloyal: anticlimactic actions, ineffectiveness, powerless danger

XVI • DISASTER

This card comes in closely to the next three cards, creating a grouping of concepts that tie into the end of the rising action and conflict of the story.

Starting off the set, disaster is a result of the character's choices up to this point and the influence of the antagonist. Setbacks and consequences must, at some point within the story, lead to disaster. This is the point in the story where all seems lost and the character is at their lowest low. This event destroys all their hopes and all their careful preparations, leaving them with nothing.

When everything collapses on the protagonist how do they respond? What measures do they take to try to weather the disaster?

This phase should put them in survival mode, which should show the reader just who they are in an emergency. This should be the beginning of the trial that sets them on the path to the final battle with the antagonist.

Loyal: darkness, despair, loss, anomie, deconstruction, metanoia

Disloyal: hope, insight, revelation, illumination, rescue

XVII • DOUBT

When everything comes crashing down, the character is called to question everything they believed in about themselves and the world they know. When this doubt sets in, the character experiences a dark night of the soul, in which they doubt everything around them and even the truth and worthiness of their existence.

This phase is not just good for tension and plot, it's good for character building. We don't often see what kind of a person the character is until they've hit rock bottom. What is the worst day of your character's life? How do they try to cope? What does their doubt and despair show about them? What have they lost and what are they most afraid to lose? What is the one thing that would push them past the point of no return?

When they doubt themselves and their world, the character reveals not only what they fear most, but also what is the most important to them. This may even come as a surprise to them, leading to what could be an epiphany, or making them delve deeper into the worst time of their lives. Also consider what has the power to do this to them, to take away everything that would have given them hope.

Working on this aspect of the character and the story can lead to deeper understanding of the character's motivations, world, and understanding of their lives.

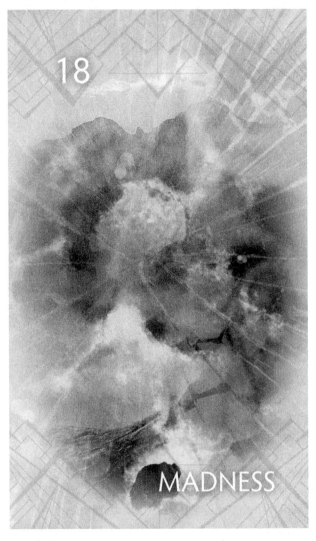

Loyal: depression, rage, coping mechanisms, detachment, distancing

Disloyal: solace, grounding, perspective

XVIII • MADNESS

When a character experiences the worst moment of their lives, it is understandable if they go mad. Sometimes this is shown in a bar, with the character drinking with their despair. Other times it's shown in a berserker rage, where they destroy everything around them in order to get back the one thing they have lost forever. However your character responds, madness is likely a part of their coping mechanism.

Although there are clichéd ways to do this, there are also reasonable ways that a person can be expected to respond to everything in their life going wrong .Whether this is from a literal antagonist, from an external force that has destroyed their lives (such as a hurricane), or even their own mind ruining everything they have ever worked for.

Take into account what madness looks like when it is a reasonable response to stressors that should break your character. Whatever this madness, remember that it only need last as long as it takes for your character to learn the skills necessary to overcome it.

When writing a character, the three phases of disaster, doubt, and madness are all parts of the emotional plot line that must be resolved before the external conflict can be overcome. The character must come out from these phases stronger if they are to be the hero of their own story.

Loyal: re–prioritization, focus, realization, sunrise

Disloyal: fog, doubt, obscurity, misdirection, incorrect conclusions

XIX • CLARITY

Even after the darkest night, the sun must always rise. The binge ends, the madness fades, clarity returns to the soul of the beleaguered character. This may happen before the conflict, or in the midst of the conflict when the character has the realization that will give them the confidence they need, the hope to help them overcome that one last obstacle that is keeping them from victory.

This is the part of the story where the music starts, the theme song that the character has had throughout the story, but that has faded and grown quiet in the previous cards.

This moment is when the character returns with all of their previous experiences, all of their knowledge, all of the hard–won skills they have learned from the beginning of the book until this moment. This is when the character triumphs over their madness and defeats their inner demons.

When writing this scene, be sure to give them this genuine moment of confidence, the much needed inner victory that can herald an outer one. Even if the character doesn't defeat the antagonist and win the day, they have at least won this moment.

What does your character's moment of clarity look like? What do they need to give them to confidence to believe they can win?

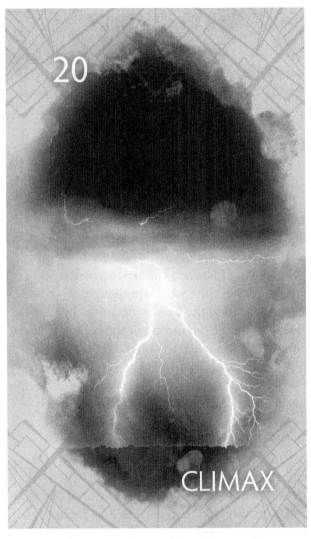

Loyal: height of conflict, summit of the plot arc

Disloyal: false climax, nonsensical climax, flat climax

XX • CLIMAX

This is the minute, the second, the tables turn and the character has a chance to overcome the antagonist. Whether they do or not is determined by the tools they've received in their journey, the knowledge, the guide, balance, and so forth. Consider whether they have been provided with the tools for the job, and what they are. Sometimes they may not even be the things you or the character thinks they might be.

When writing this scene, take into account everything that has happened so far. This point must have been coming for a long time, perhaps not explicitly, but implicitly throughout the story. This point, and no other in this novel, must be the critical point where the character must triumph or lose everything.

This is the resolution of the main conflict, the external conflict. Only by conquering inner conflict in the previous card can the character emerge strong enough to overcome the outer conflict.

Finally, this is final iteration of the try/fail where they will finally overcome the worst thing that can happen to them. Keep in mind that this may be a relatively small thing that destroys the world as they know it or large enough to destroy the entire world, beyond their own personal sphere.

21

RESOLUTION

Loyal: peace, aftermath, conclusions, farewells

Disloyal: loose ends, unbelievable results, unexpected fall out, unresolved endings

XXI • RESOLUTION

This is the end, the point of the story where everything is neatly wrapped up and the world can go on its way. The surviving characters pause and look around themselves to find they have, after all, survived to some degree. This is where the dead are mourned, the living are celebrated, and the antagonist is gone, either defeated or dead.

When writing this last part of your story (no matter when you've actually written it, some authors write their resolution first), consider how you want to wrap up your story. What last impression do you want to leave your readers with? How do you want to resolve the mystery that was set up at the beginning of the novel? What ending best represents the theme and the characterization? How best is the plot ended to give the reader the most satisfaction?

Remember when writing this that the ending is just as important as the beginning. This is the part that may encourage your reader to pick up your book again. If the ending is satisfying, it makes the entire book worth it.

The climax may reveal the meaning of the mystery, but the resolution concludes it, drawing the curtains on the story and letting the characters take a final bow. Consider how you would like your story to end and write that ending. If it is a series, consider how to write the hook for the next volume.

THE MINOR ARCANA

The Minor Arcana represent the smaller aspects of life, traits of the character, basis of the conflicts, stages of character development, professions or aspects that the character can have ascribed to them. These cards hold less explicit weight in the story than the Major Arcana, but still provide vital insight into the characters' experience. As with the Major Arcana, the Minor Arcana can be read both disloyal and loyal.

Each suit has a specific meaning, an overall theme particular to each. Keys represent thought and mind–related concepts. Pens represent forms of conflict. Pages represent emotions. Clocks represent sensations and aspects of the physical world.

Aces represent beginnings of things. When these come up, think of how things start. Think of the inception of thoughts and conflicts, the beginning of emotional states, the origin of sensations.

ACE OF KEYS
THOUGHT

Consider what knowledge the character is beginning to understand. What thoughts are just starting in the character's mind that can lead to future outcomes? What new thought has occurred to them that can affect the current situation?

ACE OF PENS
CONFLICT

This card can indicate the beginning of a conflict. Or the renewal of an old one. What battle has begun in your character's world that is indicated by this card? Is this conflict internal or external? How does this conflict affect the current situation and the larger plot?

ACE OF PAGES
EMOTION

With this card comes the start of a new emotion. Which emotion makes the most sense in this situation? Is it the one that is the most obvious, or is it more nuanced than that? What emotion is the one that resonates the most in this part of the story?

ACE OF CLOCKS
SENSATION

Vital to every story is physical sensation. What sensations are your character experiencing? What new thing have they felt, tasted, smelled, seen, or heard? Describe their experiences vibrantly so the reader can feel them as well.

Twos represent balance between opposing or kindred forces, the world in equilibrium for a moment. Look at the way the elements in your story interact and find those perfect moments of balance to describe. They are coordinated with the threes, in opposition or in sequence.

TWO OF KEYS
STUDY

When examining this card, consider what the character is learning and what they can bring into their lives. How do they find the balance between external stimuli and internal thought? What skills do study give to the character?

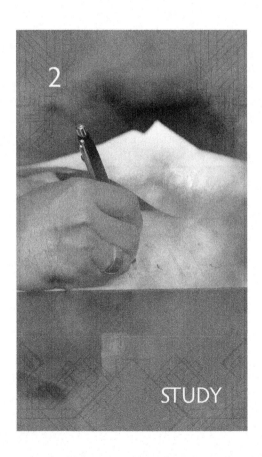

TWO OF PENS
TRAINING

In preparing for any sort of conflict, training is necessary. What sort of training has your character gone through? What have they experienced that has given them the skills necessary to fight?

TWO OF PAGES
PASSION

What is your character's passion in life? What drives them? What keeps their heart in balance? This, like so many of the other cards, has the potential of being unbalanced as much as the others, but this one can often have deeper repercussions, as the heart is often the most hard to realign after it has been placed out of whack.

TWO OF CLOCKS
PLEASURE

What can bring more balance, more sense of wellness, to our lives than pleasure? What does your character find pleasurable? Do they seek out this pleasure when they need balance? Or does the pleasure itself unbalance them?

THREE

The threes and twos find each other in that they are either the completion or the opposite of the other. The threes can be the representation of too much of a good thing within the suit.

THREE OF KEYS
EXAMINATION

At the end of every study period comes examination. No matter whether your character is formally or informally studying, the day will come when their knowledge must be put to the test. Are they prepared for this test? Or have they been lax in their studies? What knowledge will contribute to their success here?

EXAMINATION

THREE OF PENS
INDOCTRINATION

With every kind of training comes a certain level of indoctrination. What country, cause, or issue is your character willing to fight for? What has caused them to be so willing to fight for what they believe in? What indoctrination (for good or for ill) have they experienced that grounds their certainty?

THREE OF PAGES
HATE

In contrast to passion, there is always hate. What does your character hate? Do they despise it or is it merely an annoyance? What level of hate corresponds to their passions? What would they do with that hate?

THREE OF CLOCKS
PAIN

Experiencing even pleasure to an extreme can bring pain. How does your character deal with pain? What kind of pain can get through the chinks in their armor to truly hurt them? Are they weak or strong when presented with pain? What will it take to break them?

FOUR

Fours speak to stability, with the four points of anything providing a stable structure from which to grow. A chair is stable, a car is stable, and so forth. From this stability, the character can move forward into the story.

FOUR OF KEYS
APPLICATION

How do they apply their knowledge? The character has passed the point of balance and now must utilize their skills to conquer practical problems in the real world. What does this application look like? How can they best use their knowledge to solve the problem at hand? Do they have the understanding to use their knowledge in a practical application?

APPLICATION

FOUR OF PENS
FIGHTING

After training and indoctrination, the character must use their skills to fight. How do they choose to do so? In what arena do they combat? Do they have the discretion yet to use their skills to fight and win?

FOUR OF PAGES
FEAR

Fear is an emotion that sparks more useful responses than any other emotion. Through fear we can learn what is dangerous and poses a threat. Does your character have enough control over their emotions to learn what to wisely fear? Do they have the strength yet to fight through that fear if necessary? Or does the fear control them completely?

FOUR OF CLOCKS
THE SENSES

Through these senses we seek understanding of the world around us. What does your character sense? Are they using one sense more than the others? How do the senses play out in the story and build it up? What can the character make use of more in this story or scene to better illustrate it to the reader?

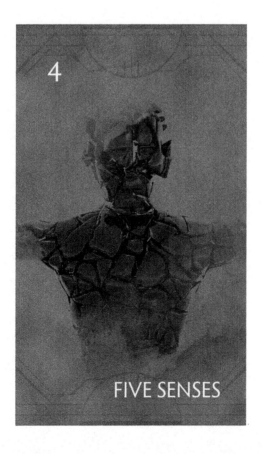

FIVE

Fives start the conflict cards. Although there are traditionally four to eight different kinds of conflict in stories, this deck breaks them down into each suit, giving a total of twelve conflicts to inform your story. These don't necessarily have to be the primary conflict, but if they are, consider all facets of their consequences.

FIVE OF KEYS
CHARACTER VS. BODY

Oftentimes the mind fights against the body. What about your character prevents them from seeing their body as the vessel they desire to propel them through life? What conflict can arise between their sense of self and their outward presentation of self?

FIVE OF PENS
CHARACTER VS. TECHNOLOGY

Technology has been with humanity since the beginning of societies from the first stick to the latest smart device. How does your character fight against technology? What about technology makes their lives harder or makes their lives more complex? Are there particular technologies that arise to obstruct your character's path?

FIVE OF PAGES
CHARACTER VS. CHEMISTRY

Brain chemistry can be the hardest thing for someone to combat, pitting a character's mind against itself. Chemical imbalances cause mental illness, visions, nightmares, even other disorders throughout the body. How do these present in your character's world? How do they hinder them and prevent them from achieving their goal?

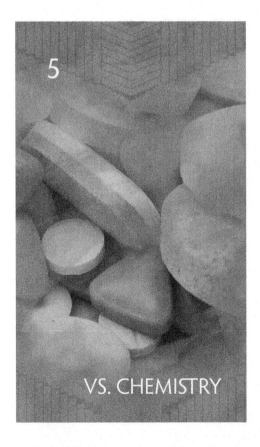

FIVE OF CLOCKS
CHARACTER VS. DISEASE

The external world is also fraught with conflict. Has your character struggled with disease? Have they lost someone due to disease? Has it prevented them from being able to achieve the things they wanted to due to its debilitating nature?

SIX

Sixes continue the conflict series, deepening the stakes and consequences. Keep in mind that the character doesn't always need to win in the long term, just in the short term.

SIX OF KEYS
CHARACTER VS. MIND

Even when chemical imbalances don't interfere, the mind can be a formidable opponent. Our own doubts and fears belay our ability to succeed in life and can have disastrous effects if we do not somehow overcome them. With this card, ask what the character fears most from their own mind. What is their greatest challenge when facing themselves?

SIX OF PENS
CHARACTER VS. PERSON

Other people can be our worst enemies as well. What person stands as the signifier of this conflict in your character's life? What power does that person have to stand in as an opponent and a form of conflict? Who are they to challenge your character?

SIX OF PAGES
CHARACTER VS. GODS

No matter the character's religion, the gods may have an effect on the conflict. Even if this card can be translated as "forces greater than the character" this conflict stands. How can a character fight against something like this? From what well of strength do they draw to overcome this challenge?

SIX OF CLOCKS
CHARACTER VS. TIME

When fighting against time, time always wins in the end. However, how can your character win in this story, in this moment? Do they beat the clock? Say the last word? How do they fight against the imposing nature of time on our lives? How can they win?

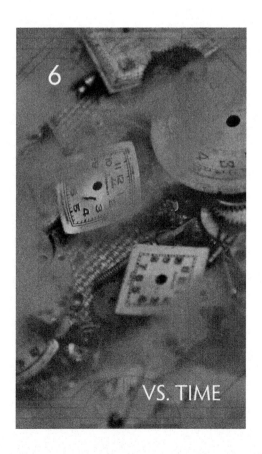

SEVEN

Sevens conclude the conflicts, making them personal. When writing these sorts of conflicts, consider how your character's inner and outer conflicts relate to them.

SEVEN OF KEYS
CHARACTER VS. ADDICTION

One of the hardest things to overcome is an addiction. What is your character addicted to? Is it a common addiction (television, drugs, cigarettes, alcohol)? Or is it something, or someone, else? Is it something they are willing to give up? Is it something they have the strength to?

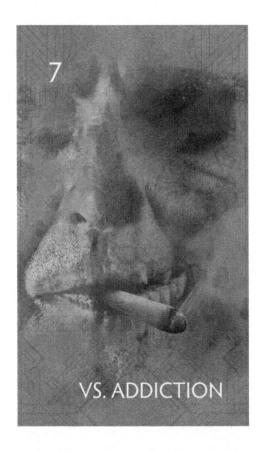

SEVEN OF PENS
CHARACTER VS. LAWS

Unless your character is a paragon of lawfulness, they have broken some laws. Do they speed? Smoke within twenty feet of a building? Litter? Or are their rule–breaking actions less trivial? Even if they haven't broken any laws how do their personal values align with the laws of their culture?

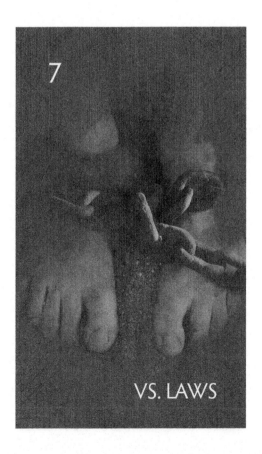

SEVEN OF PAGES
CHARACTER VS. CULTURE

Culture can be an opposing force to your character's wants and needs. How does your character fit into their culture? What oppositional tendencies do they possess? How do they respond to the demands of other people's codes of conduct on their lives, and the code of conduct they live by?

SEVEN OF CLOCKS
CHARACTER VS. NATURE

Despite the tendency in our society to ignore nature, consider it quaint, or even frightening, nature is an active force in our everyday lives. It governs what we wear, what we do and even how we do it. How does nature play into your character's life and make it more difficult? How do they react to nature? How does it ruin their lives in particular?

EIGHT

Eights frame and lead up to the concepts in the nines while still remaining forces in and of themselves. They frame the context of the character in the narrative of the darker, more desperate aspects of human emotion.

EIGHT OF KEYS
RELUCTANCE

When considering the character's thought processes with this card, consider all aspects of the emotion. What are they avoiding? What are they trying not to do, be, or think about? What do they think about instead?

EIGHT OF PENS
RAGE

Although an emotion, rage deals with how the character can relate to the conflicts in their lives. What enrages them? What makes them so angry that they can barely speak? How do they present this anger?

EIGHT OF PAGES
GUILT

Everyone has secrets and secret guilts. What does your character feel guilty about? How do they deal with guilt? Do they hide it as deep as it will go and try not to think about it? Do they reveal it for everyone? Are they forced to deal with it by outside forces?

EIGHT OF CLOCKS
BARGAINING

One of the ways in which people deal with issues in their lives is by bargaining. What do they bargain for? How do they strive to strike a deal? With whom are they bargaining? How good of a bargainer are they?

NINE

Nearing the end of the numbered cards, we come to the same place in the suit as we do with the Major Arcana: the dark night of the soul, the end of things where everything is full of despair. These may be on a more minor scale, but no less important to the character's journey.

NINE OF KEYS
DENIAL

When reluctance no longer works, denial can often be an end result. What does the character refuse to think about? What are they denying in their lives? Is it something like love or something like hate? What do they refuse?

NINE OF PENS
WAR

The end–result of conflict when diplomacy fails is war, either on a small scale or a large one. How does this present in your character's life? Is it a literal or figurative war? What do they care so much about that they would let it get to this point? What has brought them to this stage in their journey?

NINE OF PAGES
DEPRESSION

This is the literal dark night of the soul, the worst place someone can be emotionally. What has sent your character here? How do they deal with being here? Or do they not deal at all? How can they get out of this place?

NINE OF CLOCKS
DESPERATION

Once bargaining fails, desperation comes next. What is your character desperate for? What prevents them from reaching this goal? What do they want so badly that they find themselves in this place?

TEN

Nines are the epitome of the suit, the end–result of every card that has led up to this point. They also are the point in which the character rises out of the despair of the nines and overcomes the difficulties they are facing.

TEN OF KEYS
EPIPHANY

The end point of thought is epiphany, the final break through to the completeness of thought and form that the character strives for. What is your character's epiphany? How do they seek to achieve it? What thought processes go through to make this end–result possible?

TEN OF PENS
PEACE

After war comes peace. What does peace look like to your character? What do they find after the end of the conflict? What do they want most and how is this reflected in the peace they find?

TEN OF PAGES
HAPPINESS

Emotionally, happiness in one form or another is the end result of the character's emotional journey—their goal. What does happiness look like to your character? Is it what they thought it would be? Does it satisfy them or do they look for more?

TEN OF CLOCKS
SUCCESS

Success comes in all forms, and the character's success may look different even to them. How do they measure success? Have they achieved that point? Is this a final success, or a stepping stone to the next venture?

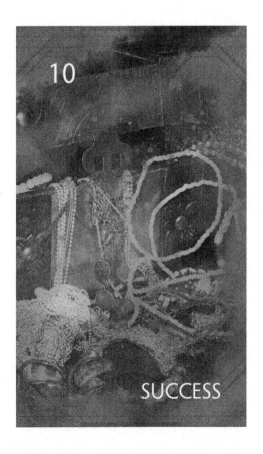

THE COURT CARDS

The court cards represent people in their different roles and concepts that apply to these. Starting with pages, the progression becomes increasingly complex as the characters grow in responsibility and maturity. These cards, when read, can represent either the character themselves, or a member of the supporting cast that has some influence on the character's situation. Also consider how these cards can transcend gender barriers and be reflected in people from all genders.

PAGE

As the first of the court cards, pages represent beginners, much like the aces represent beginnings. Consider when writing these characters how they start out and how they can grow from their place in the world.

PAGE OF KEYS
STUDENT

Students start with little knowledge, and grow as they progress. How is your character a student? What do they learn in their journey? What do they need to study to progress from this phase?

PAGE OF PENS
ADVENTURER

With any adventure, someone must embark on that journey. How does your character begin their adventure? What form do they take as the adventurer? How do they grow fromt his stage?

PAGE OF PAGES
SIDEKICK

This card may also be considered the understudy. Is this character a sidekick in that they never grow to be a hero in their own right? Or are they satisfied playing a support role? How does this play into their sense of self?

PAGE OF CLOCKS
SERVANT

A person can be a servant to anything in their lives. How does your character play the part of a servant? How do they serve their goals, their needs, the needs of others, their community? How do they view this aspect of their lives? Do they resent or respect it?

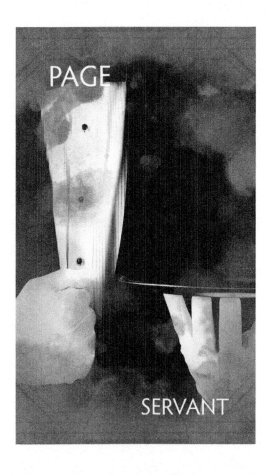

Knights represent forward motion in the story. These characters draw on the concepts of action and movement to illustrate their natures.

KNIGHT OF KEYS
LIBRARIAN

The librarian moves the literal representations of thought, books, from one place to the next, organizing and collating them into a form that makes them easily retrievable. How does your character embody these aspects of thought? How do they organize their consciousness and thoughts to better understand the world around them?

KNIGHT OF PENS
CRUSADER

This character fights for their cause, their beliefs. What is your character willing to fight for? What do they believe in so strongly that they will take a stand for it? How is this fight embodied in their lives?

KNIGHT OF PAGES
CAMPAIGNER

Like the crusader, the campaigner stands for what they believe in. However, unlike the crusader, this character persuades rather than battles. How is our character persuasive? Are they capable of doing so and swaying others to their cause? What resources do they bring to bear on the problem at hand?

KNIGHT OF CLOCKS
DEFENDER

This character not only stands for their cause, but is willing to defend it. While this may seem less active than the other Knights, it is still a means of movement. What does your character want to defend? How do they defend the things the love and believe in? What does this look like in the story?

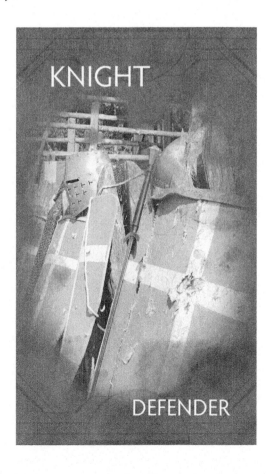

QUEEN

Queens represent the counseling and informative aspects of the suit. These characters are the ones that take the nature of the suit and use it in a less active form than the knights, but instead as a tool rather than a weapon.

QUEEN OF KEYS
TEACHER

Teachers bring knowledge to others, building thought processes and helping them find new ways of considering information. When writing this sort of character, consider their kind of expertise. What are they best geared to teach? How do they teach? Do they have all the skills to convey the information they must?

QUEEN OF PENS
SWASHBUCKLER

When writing this character, consider how they use the concepts of danger and adventure to their lives. A swashbuckler is somewhat of a daredevil, using their knowledge of the conflict to their advantage. How does your character operate within the conflict? Do they have the skills to navigate it safely and with panache? How do they regard the nature of the conflict?

QUEEN OF PAGES
MEDIATOR

Arguments can be emotional and this is where this queen comes into play. As the mediator, this character navigates the treacherous emotional nature of the conflict. How do they manage to negotiate the pitfalls of emotional issues? How do they use their emotional intelligence to mediate situations?

QUEEN OF CLOCKS
CONSUL

This character is someone, like an ambassador, who moves from one realm to another to negotiate for the benefit of those they are charged with protecting. What realms does your character move through? How do they navigate between them while still protecting their interests and those of the people they care about?

KING

Kings represent the staid force of the suit embodied in a character. This is the epitome of the concept of the suit, the end–result of a hard–fought journey to the top. These characters also have more responsibility and are integral to holding together the concept.

KING OF KEYS
PROFESSOR

This person is considered to have the epitome of knowledge on a subject, and is an expert in their field. What does your character have expertise in? What are they the best at? What knowledge do they know to the degree that they could be considered the best in their field?

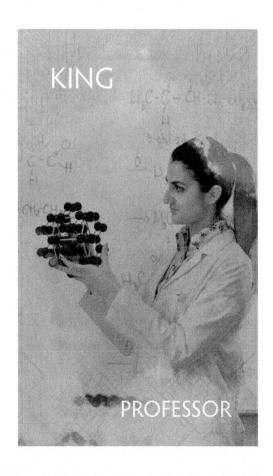

KING OF PENS
LEADER

Although any form of military rank could represent this card, the concept of the leader best represents the epitome of the conflict suit. How does your character lead? What do they lead? Do they inspire others to follow?

KING OF PAGES
POLITICIAN

A politician is someone who serves the people, but it is not unknown for them to serve themselves more. How does your character seek to govern? Do they rule wisely? Do they use their power for selfish aims? Or are they true to their beliefs and their emotions?

KING OF CLOCKS
BOSS

This person is the most successful in their field, nominated to be in charge of others and responsible for the finances of a company. How does your character deal with this accountability? Can their responsibility be considered literal or figurative in their situation? How do they handle these goals and charges?

SPREADS

This section deals with the previously mentioned spreads and also provides examples of how I would use the cards in a reading. Note that I follow the sense of the cards, the connotation, rather than the denotation in some cases. Partly this is because of how I want the story to go, and also partly it is because of how I see the cards interacting with each other. Feel free to use this method in your own reading, letting the cards speak to each other through the spread and tell a story through their combined meanings, rather than looking at each card singly.

PAST · PRESENT · FUTURE
BASIC THREE CARD SPREAD

Deal three cards to represent the past influence, the current factor, and the possible outcome of the situation. This is a pretty versatile spread as it can be applied to many questions and problems within the narrative.

An example of the three card spread is as follows.

1 – Past: Indoctrination

2 – Present: VIII Consequences (r)

3 – Future: XI Strength

In this reading, the character is indoctrinated in the past, has to deal with those consequences in the present (but in a way that damages them, because the card is disloyal) and comes away from it stronger in the future.

RELATIONSHIP SPREAD

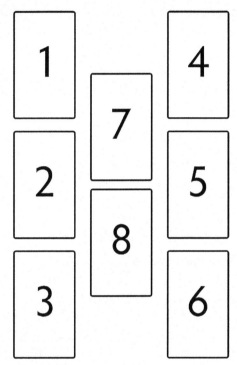

CHARACTER 1'S COLUMN:
1 – Past
2 – Present
3 – Future

CROSSING COLUMN:
7 – Present Situation
8 – Outcome

CHARACTER 2'S COLUMN:
4 – Past
5 – Present
6 – Future

In this spread, deal the cards out in the order above, then read them for the characters in order, examining the aspects of each one's life in turn before going to the middle to see how they match up.

Card 1: Character vs. Time (6 of Clocks)

Card 2: V Status Quo

Card 3: Conflict (Ace of Pens) (r)

Card 4: Happiness (10 of Pages)

Card 5: III Growth

Card 6: II Mystery

Card 7: Librarian (Knight of Keys) (r)

Card 8: Study (2 of Keys)

In this spread, one character has spent their past fighting against time (Six of Clocks) only now to find themselves up against the status quo (V). Their future conflicts, if they cannot resolve their feelings about how things are, are likely to start only to fail (Ace of Pens).

The second character's past involves the epitome of happiness. (10 of Pages) Now they are experiencing a period of growth based on that happiness (III). Their future is governed by a mystery that leads the character to the present situation (II). When these two characters meet, it is in a library, likely by the first character making noise to express their disapproval of their situation. In order to resolve the problem, both characters must work together and find an outcome.

CELTIC CROSS SPREAD

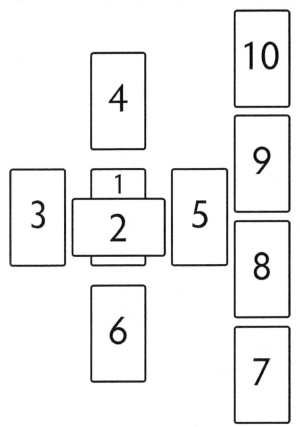

1 – Main Character
2 – Opposing factor / Challenge
3 – Past influences
4 – Present factors / Consequences
5 – Future projections / Future outcomes
6 – Underlying causes / Subconscious elements
7 – As they see themselves / Advice
8 – As others see them / External Influences
9 – Hopes and fears
10 – Outcome

This spread resembles a story in that it outlines a journey from inception to conclusion. When using this spread, look at each card as building on the next and in relation to each other. Each should build from the first part to the very end.

The second example uses the Celtic Cross ten card spread:

Card 1:   Student (Page of Keys)

Card 2:   Desperation (9 of Clocks)

Card 3:   Examination (3 of Keys)

Card 4:   VIII Consequence

Card 5:   Character vs. Addiction (7 of Keys)

Card 6:   Pain (3 of Clocks)

Card 7:   XVI Doubt

Card 8:   Application (4 of Keys)

Card 9:   Sensation (Ace of Clocks)

Card 10: XXI Resolution

In this spread, I shuffled and thought about starting a new story. With that frame of mind, I looked at the cards as dealt to tell a story in itself. The story begins with a student (Page of Keys), challenged by desperation (Nine of Clocks). In the past they have had a test (Examination) that they were desperate about, to the point of experiencing physical pain, perhaps an ulcer (Three of Clocks). In the present they have to face up to the consequences of their actions in the past that lead to a future of addiction. I read this as they cheated on their test in the past, and now they have the danger of becoming addicted to cheating on subsequent tests once they see how successful they are with this one.

The advice they were given has led them to doubt (XVI) their course of action, and others have been telling them to apply themselves more (Four of Keys). Their hopes and fears are the return of the pain that pushed them to cheat in the first place (Ace of Clocks). The outcome is the resolution (XXI) of the initial concepts that they will have to deal with the consequences of their actions, no matter whether they continue their course of action or not.

Notice the difference between the three card spread and the Celtic Cross spread. The larger the spread the greater the depth and complexity.

WORLDBUILDING SPREAD

8	**1**	**2**
7	**9**	**3**
6	**5**	**4**

1 – City
2 – Government
3 – Religion
4 – Occupation
5 – Social Class
6 – Culture
7 – Artistic Values
8 – Public Works
9 – Character's place within society

The Writer's Block Tarot can be used to develop the worldbuilding aspects of writing a novel as well. When using this spread, consider the exterior elements of your writing, pulling it past the page so that it bleeds off the edges of the book's reality. This spread is based on the eight aspects of civilization to draw the characters into the society that surrounds them. Each card placement should tell you something about the character's place in society, ending in the card that sums up their experience. The titles for each spread are not meant to be exclusive of other types of that same thing (such as a city can be a town, a village, a settlement, a space station, etc). Two examples follow.

Card 1:   Character vs. Time (6 of Clocks)
Card 2:   Training (2 of Pens)
Card 3:   XIV Balance
Card 4:   Depression (9 of Pages)
Card 5:   Consul (Queen of Clocks)
Card 6:   Teacher (Queen of Keys)
Card 7:   Character vs. Culture (7 of Pages) (r)
Card 8:   War (9 of Pens)
Card 9:   Defender (Knight of Clocks)

In this reading, the society described is one that has old cities (Six of Clocks) and a new government (2 of Pens). The religion is based on Balance (XIV) and may involve two deities or a deity and an antagonist. The character is not happy about what they do (Nine of Pages) and this likely has to do with their social status (Queen of Clocks).

The culture tends to look at their place as that of the Queen of Keys, which can creates a sense of anomie when it comes to their position in society. The artistic values are stagnant or anti-culture (7 of Pages) and their public works are based around war (Nine of Pens). Therefore the character finds themselves in a place where they become the defender of what they believe in in a society that is crumbling and unstable around them (Knight of Clocks).

Card 1: Character vs. Disease (5 of Clocks) (r)

Card 2: The Senses (4 of Clocks) (r)

Card 3: Character vs. Technology (5 of Pens)

Card 4: III Growth

Card 5: Defender (Knight of Clocks)

Card 6: Pleasure (2 of Clocks)

Card 7: Character vs. Time (6 of Clocks)

Card 8: I Knowledge (r)

Card 9: Protagonist (r)

This reading involves a lot of reversed cards, and as such is a good example of how to read them. In this society, disease has become a thing of the past (Five of Clocks) and the senses govern how people live their lives in a hedonistic society (Four of Clocks). The religion speaks against this technology, but the character may not care given their struggle with this religion. The character's job has something to do with growth (III), which they might find difficult in a society that is hedonistic and stagnant. Instead they are viewed as a defender (Knight of Clocks) of the way things are and may be involved in maintaining the status quo of hedonism on a minor level (2 of Clocks). The artistic values harken to older times, and a revival is occurring in the artistic sphere (6 of Clocks). Pubilc works actively have nothing to do with knowledge or the furtherance of the same and likely intellectualism is frowned upon (I). The character then finds themselves as someone who doesn't fit into what their culture expects of their protagonist in this place within their society. The reversed protagonist (O) might indicate the severe dissatisfaction with the way things are and the desire to change them.

WRITER'S BLOCK TAROT SPREAD

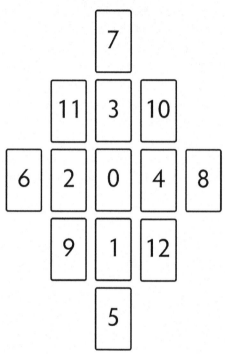

0 – Character
1 – Underlying factors
2 – Internal Past
3 – Internal Present
4 – Internal Future
5 – External Past
6 – External Present
7 – External Future
8 – Outcome
9 – Internal Desires
10 – Internal Worldview
11 – External Views of Other People
12 – External Influences (Worldbuilding)

Using thirteen cards, this spread is more extensive than many, but this allows you to get into a deeper level of detail for your story than otherwise. Note that there are two dimensions to this spread, an internal axis and an external axis. These are sometimes referred to as the "B" plot line (internal) and the "A" plot line (external). In order for the external conflict to be resolved, the internal issues the character experiences must be resolved first.

Card 0:   VII Journey (r)

Card 1:   Bargaining (8 of Clocks)

Card 2:   War (9 of Pens) (r)

Card 3:   XV Antagonist (r)

Card 4:   Politician (King of Pages) (r)

Card 5:   Sensation (Ace of Clocks)

Card 6:   Professor (King of Keys)

Card 7:   The Senses (4 of Clocks) (r)

Card 8:   Mediator (Queen of Pages) (r)

Card 9:   XVII Doubt

Card 10:   XVI Disaster (r)

Card 11:   Epiphany (10 of Keys) (r)

Card 12:   VII Consequence

Here the character is going on a journey or expedition (VII), or have been bargaining in order to go on a journey (Eight of Clocks). Internally, war is either just beginning or has been going on for long enough that it's an ongoing, exhausting conflict (Nine of Pens). This character feels that another character who is barring their progress is an antagonist, but they may be incorrect in this since that person might be looking out for their best interests (XV). Instead that person might be the politician they need to help them in the future, someone they might not want to make an enemy of (King of Pages).

Externally, In the past they have been new at experiencing their senses, trained, perhaps, to ignore them by their profession. In the present, they have become a professor, someone who has enough skill to teach at a high level and well versed in knowledge (King of Keys). Now they must rely on their senses to keep them going in the future, something they are not yet accomplished with doing, which will prove frustrating to them (Four of Clocks). The outcome will come at the hands of a mediator, someone who can help them overcome their difficulties and see the other characters for who they are, not who the protagonist views them as being, but they are likely not to listen to this person (Queen of Pages).

Their doubts have crippled them internally (XVII) and have made them view everything as an unrecoverable disaster (XVI). Other people expect them to come to an epiphany, that they must come to one given the influences on them, and yet the character does not (Ten of Keys). Therefore they must deal with the consequences of their shortsightedness and inability to function due to the perceptions informed by the inner conflict.

Card 0:   Desperation (9 of Clocks)

Card 1:   Rage (8 of Pens) (r)

Card 2:   Epiphany (10 of Keys) (r)

Card 3:   VII Journey (r)

Card 4:   Character vs. Mind (6 of Keys) (r)

Card 5:   Reluctance (8 of keys)

Card 6:   Professor (King of Keys)

Card 7:   X Try/Fail Cycle (r)

Card 8:   Emotion (Ace of Pages)

Card 9:   Mediator (Queen of Pages (r)

Card 10:   Teacher (Queen of Keys)

Card 11:   Guilt (8 of Pages) (r)

Card 12:   Success (10 of Clocks) (r)

The story here begins with the character in desperation (Nine of Clocks). Rage has failed them, sputtering out before it fully caught (Eight of Pens) and their epiphany has disappeared like a dream (Ten of Keys). Now they must go on a journey of self discovery, but aren't handling it very well (VII), instead losing the fight against their own mind (Six of Keys). In the past others have been reluctant to help them (Eight of Keys) and now their closest confidant now, an expert in their field, is the only person they can rely on (King of Keys). But without overcoming these issues, they will be eternally in the try/fail cycle, unable to break free (X). This is a battle of emotions, one that they must win in order to succeed (Ace of Pages). Their internal desires are to mediate these swelling emotions within them (Queen of Pages), but they don't know how even though they see themselves as a teacher in this very field (Queen of Pages). But emotional intelligence is different from learned intelligence, as this character must learn. Other people see their mental illness as guilt and treat them as such (Eight of Pages), making it hard for them to find the success they want (Ten of Clocks).

FINAL NOTES

No matter how you use this deck, I hope it helps you on your path. At the end of the day, remember that the story is yours to craft as you see fit. Use this deck in whatever manner will best help you on your path as a writer.

As always, use the tools that best serve your writing. Using this deck is a step toward growing closer to your writing and developing your proficiency with the craft.

Best of luck and happy writing!

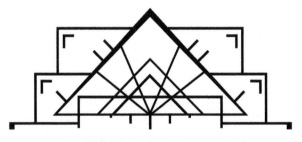

FOR FURTHER READING

The Complete Guide to the Tarot – Eden Gray

Tarot Spreads: Layouts & Techniques to Empower Your Readings – Barbara Moore

The Way of Tarot: The Spiritual Teacher in the Cards – Alejandro Jodorowsky and Marianne Costa

Tarot for Writers – Corrine Kenner

Jung and Tarot: An Archetypal Journey – Sallie Nichols

ABOUT THE AUTHOR

When not fighting crime or tinkering with Tarot spreads, Vivian Caethe writes weird fiction, science fiction, fantasy, quirky nonfiction and everything in between. She has an MFA in Creative Writing from Regis University and is a member of the Editorial Freelancer's Association. She also drinks copious amounts of tea. While doing all these things, she lives in Colorado with her super genius cat.

ABOUT THE ARTIST

After getting lost in the file trees at a very young age, Amber Peter was adopted by a pack of wild pixels, and spent her youth learning Photoshop and graphic design by cave painting. Fifteen years later, Amber is a digital jack-of-all-trades (and don't be rude...she's exceptional at them all).

WORKS CITED

Decker, Ronald, and Michael Dummett. *A History of the Occult Tarot: 1870-1970.* London: Duckworth, 2008.

Dummett, Michael. "The Double Contribution of Tarot to Popluar Culture." *In Tarot in Culture: Volume One,* by Emily E. Auger, 3-16. Valleyhome Books, 2014.

Dummett, Michael, and John McLeod. *A History of Games Played with the Tarot Pack: The Game of Triumphs. Vol. 1.* Lewston, NY: The Edwin Mellen Press, 2004.

Farley, Helen. *A Cultural History of Tarot: From Entertainment to Esotericism.* London: I.B. Tauris & Co Ltd, 2009.

Farley, Helen S. "Tarot and Egyptomania." *In Tarot in Culture Volume One,* by Emily E. Auger. Valleyhome Books.

Husband, Tim. "The Met Museum.org." *Before Fortune-Telling: The History and Structure of Tarot Cards.* April 8, 2016. http://www.metmuseum.org/blogs/in-season/2016/tarot (accessed

August 6, 2016).

Jodorowsky, Alejandro, and Marianne Costa. *The Way of Tarot: The Spiritual Teacher in the Cards.* Rochester,Vermont: Destiny Books, 2009.

Mills, Robert. "A History of the Tarot." *Byzant Tarot.* 2016. http://www.byzant.com/mystical/tarot/History.aspx (accessed 8 6, 2016).

Oatman-Stanford, Hunter. "Tarot Mythology: The Surprising Origins of the World's Most Misunderstood Cards." *Collectors Weekly. 06 18, 2014.* http://www.collectorsweekly.com/articles/the-surprising-origins-of-tarot-most-misunderstood-cards/ (accessed 08 06, 2016).

Papus. *The Tarot of the Bohemians.* Translated by A.P. Morton. London: Senate, 1994.

Place, Robert. "Iconagraphy and Allegory in Fifteenth to Seventeenth-Century Trumps." *In Tarot In Culture: Volume One*, by Emily E Auger, 17-55. Valleyhome Books, 2014.

Waite, Arthur Edward. *The Pictorial Key to the Tarot.* New York: Barnes and Noble Books, 1995.

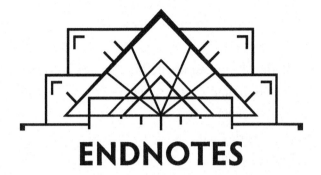

ENDNOTES

1. (Mills 2016)

2. (H. Farley 2009)

3. (Dummett and McLeod, *A History of Games Played with the Tarot Pack: The Game of Triumphs* 2004)

4. (Decker and Dummett 2008)

5. (Dummett, *The Double Contribution of Tarot to Popluar Culture* 2014)

6. (Husband 2016)

7. (Oatman-Stanford 2014)

8. (Husband 2016)

9. (Farley 2009)

10. (Farley 2009)

11. (Husband 2016)

12. (Husband 2016)

13. (Place 2014)

14. (Dummett and McLeod, *A History of Games

Played with the Tarot Pack: The Game of Triumphs 2004)

15. (Decker and Dummett 2008)

16. (Jodorowsky and Costa 2009)

17. (Decker and Dummett 2008)

18. (Place 2014)

19. (Farley 2009)(Dummett, *The Double Contribution of Tarot to Popluar Culture* 2014)

20. (Farley 2009)

21. (H. S. Farley n.d.)

22. (Farley 2009)

23. (Decker and Dummett 2008)

24. (Dummett, *The Double Contribution of Tarot to Popluar Culture* 2014)

25. (Farley 2009)

26. (Dummett, *The Double Contribution of Tarot to Popluar Culture* 2014)

27. (Papus 1994)

28. (H. Farley 2009)

29. (H. Farley 2009)

30. (Waite 1995)

CPSIA information can be obtained
at www.ICGtesting.com
Printed in the USA
LVOW04*0134151216
517286LV00006B/8/P